Smoothies, Smoothies & More Smoothies!

An Imagine Book
Published by Charlesbridge
85 Main Street, Watertown, MA 02472
617-926-0329
www.charlesbridge.com

Created by Penn Publishing Ltd.
1 Yehuda Halevi Street, Tel Aviv, Israel 65135
www.penn.co.il

Design and layout: Michal & Dekel
Editor: Shoshana Brickman
Food styling: Deanna Linder

Library of Congress Cataloging-in-Publication Data Available

ISBN 978-1-62354-031-9 (Special Edition for Barnes & Noble)

2 4 6 8 10 9 7 5 3 1

Printed in China, May 2013.

For information about custom editions, special sales, premium and corporate purchases,
please contact Charlesbridge Publishing at specialsales@charlesbridge.com

Smoothies, Smoothies & More Smoothies!

Leah Shomron & Hanni Borowski

PHOTOGRAPHY BY DANYA WEINER

imagine!
Publishing

About the Authors

Leah Shomron is a healthy-cooking culinary consultant who is dedicated to bringing awareness about healthy cooking to the public. Leah graduated from the Chef's Training program at the Natural Gourmet Institute for Health and Culinary Arts in New York. Leah writes articles, leads seminars, and has appeared on television shows, teaching people fun and easy ways to integrate healthy cooking into their lives.

Hani Borowsky is a chef who specializes in creating unique dishes for diverse audiences. She completed an internship in cooking in Tuscany, Italy, and has studied nutrition at the International College of Complementary Medicine. Hani has created menus for several bars and restaurants, and caters private events, in which several small courses are served.

Introduction

Smoothies can be so many things to so many different people. Smoothies are easy to make and fun to eat. They can be healthy or sinful, refreshing or satisfying, sweet or tangy. Smoothies can be served as a dessert, a snack, or a light meal. No matter what your mood, we're sure you'll find a smoothie to match it.

Getting Started

The first thing you need to make a great smoothie is a good blender. This means one that is strong enough to handle ice cubes, frozen fruits, crispy vegetables, and nuts. Another thing you should have is a freezer with plenty of room for storing frozen smoothie essentials, such as ice cubes, banana slices, chunks of watermelon, berries, and yogurt. If you have a selection of these items in your freezer, you'll always be able to satisfy a spontaneous smoothie craving.

The secret to making a smoothie with just the right texture is in maintaining the right proportion between solids, liquids, and frozen ingredients. The recipes in this book include just the right amount of each of these elements. If you want to make adjustments to the recipes, try to keep the ratio of elements the same. For example, if a recipe calls for 3½ oz (100 g) banana (about 1 medium fruit), and the banana you have is about 5 oz (150 g), you'll have to increase the other ingredients in the recipe (or only use part of the banana) to get the desired texture and flavor.

Making smoothies requires a bit of preparation. Many of the fresh ingredients need to be washed or peeled, and have their pits or seeds removed. If you plan on freezing ingredients, make sure you wash, peel, and chop them first. Be sure to cut fruit and nuts into relatively small chunks, since this makes things easier for your blender. Also, if you are freezing liquids, such as yogurt, do so in small-cubed ice cube tray, so that the frozen items aren't too big.

Ingredients

The size of natural ingredients such as fruits and vegetables is not uniform. To make sure you have the right texture for your smoothie, measure these ingredients in oz (g). For your convenience, cup or fruit measurements are given as well. Some of the smoothies in this book include standard ingredients such as fresh fruit, yogurt, and nuts. Others include more exotic ingredients such as nut butters and seeds. Here are a few tips about the various ingredients.

Almond butter

This protein- and calcium-rich paste, made from ground almonds, is available at health food stores and Mediterranean food stores.

Dates

Juicy, naturally sweet dates add a marvelous sweetness and texture to smoothies. Medjool dates are recommended, but may be substituted with any other dates that are sweet and flavorful.

Flax seeds

These natural seeds are high in omega-3, fatty acid, and fibers. They can be found at health food stores.

Frozen yogurt

Freeze regular, unflavored yogurt to make frozen yogurt for your smoothie. Freeze yogurt in a small-cubed ice cube tray, so that the cubes of frozen yogurt are small enough for your blender.

Fruit

Always use seedless fruit if possible, since processed seeds can make your smoothie unpleasantly bitter. If the grapes, oranges, watermelon or lemons you are using have seeds, be sure to remove them before use. Many recipes call for fresh fruit, but canned fruit can often be used instead. Just be sure to drain it well. When it comes to using apples, pears, plums, and other fruit with edible peels, I prefer to leave the peel on, but you may remove it if you like.

Granola

Adding this to a smoothie makes it thicker and crunchy. If possible, select granola made without white sugar.

Ice cream

Make sure ice cream is completely frozen before adding it to a smoothie. For ideal consistency, transfer ice cream directly from freezer to blender.

Juices

Many recipes call for fruit or vegetable juices, such as orange, carrot, lemon or celery. If you have a juicer at home, use it to make fresh juice. If not, use fresh or frozen juice from concentrate. If using readymade juice, choose ones that have no added salt or sugar.

Sugar water

This is made by combining equal amounts of brown sugar and boiling water. Stir until sugar dissolves, and then set aside to cool. Refrigerate until ready to use.

Tahini

This protein- and calcium-rich paste is made from ground sesame seeds. It may also be called sesame butter, and is often used in the Mediterranean kitchen. It's available at health food stores and Mediterranean food stores. If possible, buy tahini made from whole grain sesames.

Be Good To
Your Blender

To make a great smoothie, you need a good blender. You'll also want to take care of it. Here are some tips for making blender-friendly smoothies.

Small pieces

Cut fresh fruits and vegetables into small pieces before adding to the blender.

Small ice cubes

Use an ice cube tray with small compartments for freezing water. In these recipes, 12 small ice cubes is equal to about 1 cup of ice. We also suggest using a small-cubed ice cube tray for freezing yogurt and other liquids, so that the frozen pieces are smaller.

Liquid

You always need to have liquid in your blender before you start blending. If you like, put part of the liquid in at the beginning. Then, gradually add the rest of the liquid while the blender is operating, until the desired consistency is reached.

Help the blender

When mixing smoothies that contain frozen bananas, ice cubes, or ice, you may need to pulse the mixture a few times at the beginning. If you think something is stuck in the blender, turn it off, and use a rubber spatula to stir the ingredients a bit.

Improvising & Having Fun

Each and every one of the recipes in this book has been taste-tested. If you want to make adjustments to suit your own taste, go right ahead! Just keep the following things in mind.

Frozen agent

Every smoothie should have a frozen ingredient. If you want to replace frozen fruit with fresh fruit, you'll probably have to compensate with a few ice cubes. This will help you achieve the right texture, but the flavor might be diluted. If this happens, you may want to add sugar water or another type of sweetener.

Fruit

If you wish to replace fruit in a recipe, replace it with fruit that has a similar texture. For example, apples can be replaced with pears, and the texture will likely remain the same. However, if you replace apples with grapes, the texture of the smoothie will change, since grapes have much more liquid.

Liquids

If a recipe calls for soy milk and you have goat milk, you can probably substitute it without adjusting any of the other ingredients. If you'd like to use orange juice instead of pineapple juice, however, you may find that the other ingredients in the smoothie need to be adjusted as well. In other words, if you replace a liquid, consider whether any of the other ingredients in the smoothie should also be replaced.

Sweeteners

Many of these smoothies use sugar water for sweetening, but this can be replaced with honey, maple syrup, agave nectar, or another sweetener of your choice. If the fruit you are using is really sweet, you may not need to add any sweetener at all. Altering the amount of sweetener doesn't usually change the texture of the smoothie.

Serving Smoothies

When to serve

A smoothie should be served immediately after it is prepared. If it sits for more than few minutes, its texture and flavor are diminished.

How to serve

Technically speaking, a smoothie is a beverage and it is best served with a straw. However, you don't have to drink a smoothie. If you like, try one of these options:

— Pour the smoothie into a frozen pop container, insert a stick, and freeze it. (This is also a great way of storing extra smoothie mixture that you don't want to drink right away.)

— Pour the smoothie into an ice cream bowl, and serve with a spoon.

— Pour the smoothie into a cocktail glass, and serve with a teaspoon.

Lovingly Lemon (see recipe page 80)

Light 'n' Peachy (see recipe page 94)

Ginger Salad Smoothie (see recipe page 108)

Recipes

The recipes in this book are collected in categories according to their main ingredients. For example, healthier recipes are in the Health Boosters section; more indulgent treats are in the For Dessert section. Use these categories as guides, but don't let them limit your imagination. So roll up your sleeves, plug in your blender, and enjoy!

Classics

Pear-fectly Pink

Pear-fectly Pink

Makes 1 glass

In this smoothie, the delicately bitter flavor of pink grapefruits is balanced by the gentle sweetness of pears. Make sure you remove the grapefruit seeds before blending, since they can add an unpleasantly bitter flavor.

Ingredients

3½ oz (100 g) seeded pink grapefruit segments (about ½ medium fruit)

7 oz (200 g) pear chunks (about 2 medium fruit)

2 tablespoons sugar water (page 16)

6 small ice cubes

Preparation

In a blender, combine grapefruit, pears, sugar water, and ice. Blend until smooth.

CinnaPeach

Makes 1 glass

This smoothie is best made with ripe peaches that are rich in flavor. The addition of cinnamon adds a lovely color and aroma.

Ingredients

7 oz (200 g) white peach chunks (about 2 medium fruit)

½ cup plain yogurt

¼ cup raw cashew nuts

2 tablespoons brown sugar

Cinnamon, to taste

4 small ice cubes

Preparation

In a blender, combine peaches and yogurt.

Add cashew nuts, brown sugar, cinnamon and ice.

Blend until evenly combined.

Gingerly Ginger

Makes 1 glass

(see photo page 30)

The ginger in this smoothie gives it a lovely twist. Healthy and delicious, it's inspired by traditional cold remedies such as ginger, lemon, and honey. The addition of applesauce adds a delightful smoothness.

Ingredients

1 cup applesauce

1 teaspoon fresh ginger, peeled and grated

½ tablespoon fresh lemon juice

½ tablespoon honey

4 small ice cubes

Preparation

In a blender, combine applesauce, ginger, lemon juice, honey, and ice. Blend until smooth.

Taste of the Tropics

Makes 2 glasses

(see photo page 31)

This tropical smoothie is fresh and refreshing. Start by putting just 1 cup of coconut milk in the blender, and then add the remaining milk while the blender is running. Blend until the texture is just right.

Ingredients

1–1½ cups coconut milk

5 oz (150 g) (about 1 cup) frozen pineapple chunks

1 teaspoon fresh ginger, peeled and grated

Preparation

In a blender, combine pineapple, 1 cup coconut milk, and ginger. Blend, while gradually adding remaining coconut milk, until smooth.

Beautifully Blue

Makes 1 glass

Rich in vitamins, mineral, and fibers, blueberries are renowned for their antioxidants. Blended with bananas, this smoothie has just the right texture to serve first thing in the morning, with your favorite granola.

Ingredients

¼ cup frozen blueberries

3½ oz (100 g) frozen banana slices (about 1 medium fruit)

½ cup milk

Preparation

In a blender, combine blueberries, banana, and milk.

Blend until smooth.

Beautifully Blue

'Tis the Season

Makes 1 glass

Green apples and cranberry juice give this smoothie a tangy tartness which is perfectly softened by the maple syrup. The combination is delicious — and chock full of antioxidants!

Ingredients

7 oz (200 g) Granny Smith apple chunks
(about 2 medium fruit)

2 oz (60 g) (about ½ cup) frozen sweet berries,
such as gooseberries

⅓ cup cranberry juice

1 tablespoon maple syrup

6 small ice cubes

Preparation

In a blender, combine apples, berries, cranberry juice, maple syrup, and ice. Blend until smooth.

'Tis the season

Sweet Melon & Mint

Makes 1 glass

You can use either honeydew or cantaloupe for this recipe.
Choose the melon you like best, according to your
favorite color or what's in season.
Both types of melon are excellent with mint.

Ingredients

7 oz (200 g) (about 1½ cups) honeydew or
cantaloupe chunks

1 tablespoon chopped fresh mint or peppermint leaves

1 tablespoon honey

6 small ice cubes

Preparation

In a blender, combine melon, mint, honey, and ice.
Blend until smooth.

Sweet Melon & Mint

Gingerly Ginger (see recipe page 26)

Taste of the Tropics (see recipe page 26)

Persuasively Persimmon

Makes 1 glass

Persimmons have a relatively short season, and this sweet smoothie is a great way to make the most of them. Adding kiwi and apple produces a delicious balanced flavor.

Ingredients

7 oz (200 g) persimmon chunks (about 1–2 medium fruit)

3½ oz (100 g) kiwi chunks (about 1 medium fruit)

¼ cup applesauce

6 small ice cubes

Preparation

In a blender, combine persimmons, kiwi, applesauce, and ice. Blend until smooth.

Velvet Persimmon

Makes 1 glass

The combination of persimmons and frozen bananas gives this smoothie a particularly velvety texture. If you prefer something a bit less sweet, use Greek-style yogurt.

Ingredients

3½ oz (100 g) frozen banana slices (about 1 medium fruit)

3½ oz (100 g) persimmon chunks (about 1 medium fruit)

½ cup plain yogurt

Preparation

In a blender, combine banana, persimmon, and yogurt. Blend until smooth.

Velvet Persimmon

Vanilla Chestnut

Makes 1 glass

This smoothie is nice and simple. Make sure that the ice cream is properly frozen, and put it in the blender before the other ingredients. For a bit of extra sweetness, add 1 tablespoon of caramel syrup.

Ingredients

4 scoops vanilla ice cream

¼ cup milk

1¾ oz (50 g) roasted chestnuts, peeled and chopped

Preparation

Place ice cream and milk in a blender.

Add chestnuts, and then blend until evenly combined.

Speckled Spice

Makes 1 glass

Few things are as delicious as fresh passion fruit in season. They also lend a unique flavor and interesting texture to smoothies. This smoothie has an excellent combination of colors.

Ingredients

2½ oz (70 g) passion fruit (about 2–3 medium fruit) halved

5 oz (150 g) (about 1¼ cups) mango chunks Cinnamon, to taste

6 small ice cubes

Preparation

Scoop out contents of passion fruits and transfer to a blender. Add mango, cinnamon, and ice. Blend until smooth.

Speckled Spice

Papaya of the Caribbean

Papaya of the Caribbean

Makes 1 glass

Papaya is something of a nutritional masterpiece, thanks to its large quantity of vitamins, minerals, and fibers. Its unique flavor is perfectly complemented by banana and coconut milk.

Ingredients

3½ oz (100 g) (about ¾ cup) papaya chunks

3½ oz (100 g) frozen banana slices (about 1 medium fruit)

½ cup coconut milk

Preparation

In a blender, combine papaya, banana, and coconut milk. Blend until smooth.

Nutty Papaya

Makes 1 glass

This smoothie features the surprising yet irresistible combination of papaya, lychees, and pecans. Use fresh lychees if possible, for their fantastic flavor. If you use canned lychees, be sure to drain them well.

Ingredients

7 oz (200 g) (about 1½ cups) papaya chunks

3½ oz (100 g) (about ¾ cup) lychees, peeled and pitted

¼ cup chopped raw pecans

1 teaspoon maple syrup

6 small ice cubes

Preparation

In a blender, combine papaya, lychees, pecans, maple syrup, and ice. Blend until evenly combined.

Orange-Ginger Delight

Makes 1 glass

This bright smoothie is a great pick-me-up if you're feeling low on energy. For a more concentrated flavor, use frozen mango or cantaloupe, and omit the ice. The addition of honey and ginger gives this smoothie an unexpected twist.

Ingredients

5 oz (150 g) (about 1¼ cups) mango chunks

5 oz (150 g) cantaloupe chunks

1 tablespoon honey

1 teaspoon ginger, peeled and grated

4 small ice cubes

Preparation

In a blender, combine mango, cantaloupe, honey, ginger and ice. Blend until smooth.

Gorgeous Sweet Greens

Makes 1 glass

Kiwi is a wonderful fruit for using in smoothies, since it contributes a unique sour flavor. If you like sour drinks, you don't need to any sweetener at all. You can even replace the sugar water with lime or lemon juice, if you like.

Ingredients

7 oz (200 g) (about 2 medium) kiwi chunks

½ cup applesauce

1 tablespoon chopped fresh mint leaves

2 teaspoons sugar water (page 16), optional

4 small ice cubes

Preparation

In a blender, combine kiwis, applesauce, mint, sugar water, and ice. Blend until smooth.

Gorgeous Sweet Greens

Health Boosters

Persimmon Protein Punch

Makes 1 glass

Ingredients

1¾ oz (50 g) silk tofu

½ cup soy milk

1¾ oz (50 g) dried apricot chunks (about 5 medium fruit)

5 oz (150 g) persimmon chunks (about 1–2 medium fruit)

1 teaspoon flax seeds

1 teaspoon toasted sesame seeds

1 teaspoon maple syrup

6 small ice cubes

Preparation

In a blender, combine tofu, milk, apricots, persimmons, flax seeds, sesame seeds, maple syrup, and ice. Blend until evenly combined.

Avocado Experience

Makes 1 glass

Rich, creamy, and nutritious, avocadoes are an excellent smoothie ingredient. Be sure to serve this smoothie immediately after blending, since avocado changes color quickly once it's been chopped.

Ingredients

3½ oz (100 g) avocado chunks (about ½ medium fruit)

5 oz (150 g) pear chunks (about 1–2 medium fruit)

¼ cup applesauce

1¾ oz (50 g) pitted dried dates (about 3 large fruit)

⅓ cup water

4 small ice cubes

Preparation

In a blender, combine avocado, pears, applesauce, dates, water, and ice. Blend until smooth.

Avocado Experience

Minty Watermelon

Minty Watermelon

Makes 1 glass

You'll need a combination of frozen and fresh watermelon to get just the right texture in this smoothie. The addition of mint creates a fusion flavor that is fresh and refreshing.

Ingredients

9 oz (250 g) (about 1½ cups) frozen seedless watermelon chunks

1¾ oz (50 g) (about ⅓ cup) fresh seedless watermelon chunks

½–¾ cup water

1 tablespoon chopped fresh mint leaves

Preparation

In a blender, combine watermelon, water, and mint.

Blend until smooth.

Tropical Nut Twister

Makes 1 glass

With its combination of tropical fruit and nuts, this smoothie has an interesting texture and delicate flavor. Replace the almonds with cashews, if you like.

Ingredients

7 oz (200 g) (about 1⅓ cups) frozen pineapple chunks

5 oz (150 g) kiwi chunks (about 1½ medium fruit)

¼ cup frozen cranberries

¼ cup chopped blanched almonds

1 teaspoon brown sugar or sugar water (page 16) (optional)

Preparation

In a blender, combine pineapple, kiwi, cranberries, almonds, and brown sugar. Blend until evenly combined.

Summertime Special

Makes 1 glass

Strawberries, watermelon, and kiwis are sure signs of summer. All three are blended in this fabulous smoothie for a fresh summertime flavor. All of the fruit can be frozen in this smoothie; if you decide to use only fresh fruits, add a few small cubes of ice.

Ingredients

3½ oz (100 g) (about ¾ cup) frozen strawberries

3½ oz (100 g) kiwi chunks (about 1 medium fruit)

3½ oz (100 g) (about ¾ cup) seedless watermelon chunks

Preparation

In a blender, combine strawberries, kiwi, and watermelon. Blend until smooth.

Tutti Frutti

Makes 1 glass

With kiwi, banana, orange juice, and strawberries, this delicious smoothie is like a fresh fruit salad. Brimming with flavor and goodness!

Ingredients

3 oz (85 g) kiwi chunks (about 1 medium fruit)

3½ oz (100 g) frozen banana slices (about 1 medium fruit)

½ cup orange juice

2½ oz (75 g) (about ½ cup) frozen strawberries

Preparation

In a blender, combine kiwi, banana, orange juice, and strawberries. Blend until smooth.

Tutti Frutti

CinnaApple Almond

Makes 1 glass

Rich in fiber and calcium, almond butter makes
this smoothie extra smooth.
The cinnamon makes it fragrant.

Ingredients

1½ cups applesauce

1 tablespoon almond butter

1 teaspoon lemon zest

1 tablespoon apple juice concentrate

Cinnamon, to taste

6 small ice cubes

Preparation

In a blender, combine applesauce, almond butter,
lemon zest, apple juice concentrate, cinnamon, and ice.
Blend until smooth.

Breakfast Boost

Makes 1 glass

Rich in fiber, calcium, and protein, this smoothie makes
a great breakfast. When choosing tahini, note that tahini
made from unhulled sesame seeds contains about 5 times
more calcium than tahini made from hulled sesame seeds.

Ingredients

½ cup tahini

½ cup plain goat yogurt

½ cup rolled oats

2 tablespoons honey

4 small ice cubes or ½ cup water

Preparation

In a blender, combine tahini, yogurt, oats, honey, and ice.
Blend until smooth.

Breakfast Boost

Nourishing Nut

Makes 1 glass

This smoothie is rich in potassium, fiber, and calcium. Depending on the yogurt you choose, it may be rich in probiotics as well. If you only have frozen bananas on hand, omit the ice cubes and use just 3½ oz (100 g) of frozen bananas.

Ingredients

7 oz (200 g) sliced bananas (about 2 medium fruit)

2 tablespoons almond butter

1–2 tablespoons maple syrup

½ cup plain yogurt, preferably goat yogurt

4 small ice cubes

Preparation

In a blender, combine bananas, almond butter, maple syrup, yogurt, and ice. Blend until smooth.

Very Berry Vanilla

Makes 2 glasses

This is an absolute classic: frozen berries and vanilla yogurt. If the berries you use are quite sweet to begin with, simply omit the sugar water.

Ingredients

7 oz (200 g) (about 1½ cups) frozen berries (cranberries, raspberries, blueberries, strawberries, or blackberries)

1 cup vanilla yogurt

2 tablespoons sugar water (page 16)

Preparation

In a blender, combine berries, yogurt, and sugar water. Blend until smooth.

Very Berry Vanilla

Pomegranate Punch

Pomegranate Punch

Makes 1 glass

Pomegranate juice is flavorful, colorful, and high in vitamin C and antioxidants. If you can find pomegranates at the store, make your own juice. For a seasonal alternative, replace with cranberry juice.

Ingredients

7 oz (200 g) frozen banana slices (about 2 medium fruit)

1 cup pomegranate or cranberry juice

2 tablespoons almond butter

Preparation

Combine bananas, pomegranate juice, and almond butter in a blender. Blend until smooth.

Orange-Apricot Ambrosia

Makes 2 glasses

This nutritious smoothie is filling and flavorful, not to mention incredibly attractive. It's an excellent smoothie for ushering in apricot season.

Ingredients

7 oz (200 g) (about 1½ cups) apricot chunks

½ cup plain goat yogurt

½ cup orange juice

¼ cup chopped blanched almonds

4 small ice cubes

Preparation

In a blender, combine apricots, yogurt, orange juice, almonds, and ice. Blend until evenly combined.

Great Grape & Granola

Makes 1 glass

Flavorful, filling, and healthy, this smoothie is perfect for satisfying midmorning hunger pangs. Use red or green seedless grapes. If possible, select granola that doesn't contain white sugar.

Ingredients

6 oz (175 g) (about 1 cup) seedless grapes

½ cup granola

1 tablespoon honey

1 teaspoon flax seeds

8 small ice cubes

Preparation

In a blender, combine grapes, granola, honey, flax seeds, and ice. Blend until evenly combined.

Mediterranean Medley

Makes 1 glass

The tahini and pistachio nuts in this Mediterranean-flavored smoothie give it a nutty flavor. The figs and honey provide the sweetness, and yogurt makes it silky. It's rich in fiber, calcium, potassium, and vitamin B.

Ingredients

4 dry figs, soaked in warm water and drained

1 cup plain yogurt

¼ cup tahini

¼ cup raw shelled pistachios

1–2 tablespoons honey

6 small ice cubes

Preparation

In a blender, combine figs, yogurt, tahini, pistachios, honey, and ice. Blend until evenly combined.

Mediterranean Medley

CinnaSoy and Oats

CinnaSoy and Oats

Makes 1 glass

This smoothie combines energy, protein, and great taste. It's a great energy booster for midmorning, when you need something to tide you over until lunch. If you like, replace the raw egg white with 1 tablespoon egg white powder and 2 tablespoons water.

Ingredients

¼ cup chopped blanched almonds

¼ cup rolled oats

½ cup soy milk

3½ oz (100 g) frozen banana slices (about 1 medium fruit)

1 raw egg white

Cinnamon, to taste

Preparation

Soak almonds and oats in milk for about 30 minutes. Transfer to a blender, and add banana, egg white, and cinnamon. Blend until evenly combined.

Carobanana

Makes 2 glasses

Carob powder is a healthy alternative to chocolate. Combining it with bananas and almond milk creates a nice texture and flavor. If you like, replace the almond milk with another nut or dairy milk.

Ingredients

7 oz (200 g) frozen banana slices (about 2 medium fruit)

2 teaspoons carob powder

1 tablespoon apricot jam

1 cup almond milk

Preparation

In a blender, combine bananas, carob powder, jam, and milk. Blend until smooth.

Mango Fig-tastic

Makes 1 glass

Dairy-free yet rich in calcium and protein, this smoothie can be served as a light meal. Note that flax seeds only provide omega-3 if they have been ground, so if your blender won't grind them, use ground flax seeds instead. If you prefer this smoothie chilled, pour over 2 ice cubes to serve.

Ingredients

6 dry figs

½ cup warm water

3½ oz (100 g) silk tofu

3½ oz (100 g) (about ¾ cup) mango chunks

¾ cup soy milk, 1 tablespoon almond butter

1 tablespoon honey, 1 teaspoon flax seeds

Preparation

Soak figs in warm water for about 30 minutes. Drain figs and place in a blender. Add tofu, mango, milk, almond butter, honey, and flax seeds. Blend until combined.

It's a Date!

Makes 1 glass

Bananas and dates are a good source of fiber and potassium. Tofu adds protein, and cashews provide good fatty acids, calcium, and magnesium. Healthy and tasty!

Ingredients

3½ oz (100 g) frozen banana slices (about 1 medium fruit)

1¾ oz (50 g) silk tofu

1¾ oz (50 g) pitted dried dates (about 3 large fruit)

¼ cup chopped raw cashew nuts

1 cup soy milk

Preparation

In a blender, combine banana, tofu, dates, cashew nuts, and milk. Blend until evenly combined.

It's a Date!

Sweet & Sour Cranapple

Sweet & Sour Cranapple

Makes 1 glass

This refreshing smoothie contains antioxidants and fiber, and has lots of flavor. Note that it includes a whole fresh lemon (and not lemon juice)!

Ingredients

¼ cup frozen cranberries

2 oz (60 g) lemon (about 1 medium fruit), seeded, peeled, and chopped

1 teaspoon fresh ginger, peeled and grated

2 tablespoons honey

¼ cup applesauce

12 small ice cubes

Preparation

In a blender, combine cranberries, lemon, ginger, honey, applesauce, and ice. Blend until smooth.

Strawberry Figs Forever

Makes 1 glass

Fresh figs are in season for a very short time, and this smoothie is a great way to take advantage of them. Select granola that has no added sugar. If you can't find hazelnut milk, replace it with soy milk, cow milk, or rice milk.

Ingredients

5 oz (150 g) (about 1 cup) frozen strawberries

1¾ oz (50 g) (about 1½ cups) fresh figs, chopped

½ cup almond milk

1 ounce (30 g) (about ¼ cup) granola

Preparation

In a blender, combine strawberries, figs, almond milk and granola. Blend until evenly combined.

Low Fat/
High Flavor

Mango Date Madness

Makes 1 glass

Looking for a naturally sweet yet decadent dessert?
This smoothie is just right!

Ingredients

1 cup frozen plain yogurt

5 oz (150 g) (about 1¼ cups) mango chunks

1¾ oz (50 g) pitted dried dates (about 3 large fruit)

Preparation

In a blender, combine yogurt, mango, and dates.
Blend until smooth.

Breakfast Berry Blizzard

Makes 1 glass

Frozen yogurt gives this smoothie a magnificent texture;
the combination of apricot and blackberries makes it sweet
and refreshing. If you like, serve this smoothie in a bowl,
mixed with your favorite granola, for a delicious
breakfast for two.

Ingredients

1 cup frozen plain yogurt

1¾ oz (50 g) drained canned apricots

1¾ oz (50 g) (about ½ cup) fresh or frozen blackberries

Preparation

In a blender, combine yogurt, apricots, and blackberries.
Blend until smooth.

Breakfast Berry Blizzard

Light 'n' Peachy

Light 'n' Peachy

Makes 2 glasses

This delicious smoothie is light, fruity, and fat-free.
A pinch of cinnamon makes it a little spicy, too.
It's a great wintertime treat, since it uses canned fruit.

Ingredients

1 cup frozen fat-free plain yogurt

5 oz (150 g) drained canned peaches

1¾ oz (50 g) drained canned apricots

Cinnamon, to taste

Preparation

In a blender, combine yogurt, peaches, apricots,
and cinnamon. Blend until smooth.

Frozen Cherry Mango

Makes 1 glass

Simple but tasty, this is an easy treat to make.
It's fruity in flavor, but doesn't require any fresh fruit.

Ingredients

1 fat-free cherry frozen pop, coarsely chopped

1 fat-free mango yogurt

Preparation

In a blender, combine frozen pop and yogurt.
Blend until smooth.

Kiwi FroYo

Makes 1 glass

With sweet pears and sour kiwis, this frozen yogurt smoothie is smooth and refreshing. I prefer using pears with peels, but you can peel them, if you like.

Ingredients

1 cup frozen plain yogurt

5 oz (150 g) pear chunks (about 1–2 medium fruit)

1¾ oz (50 g) kiwi chunks (about 1 medium fruit)

Lemon zest, to taste

Preparation

In a blender, combine yogurt, pears, kiwi, and lemon zest.

Blend until smooth.

Kiwi FroYo

Tropical Yogurt Shake

Tropical Yogurt Shake

Makes 1 glass

Using orange segments rather than juice means this smoothie has more nutritional value than regular orange juice. Blended with frozen yogurt and pineapple, the result is a smoothie with an interesting texture and wonderful flavor.

Ingredients
1 cup frozen plain yogurt

3½ oz (100 g) (about ¾ cup) pineapple chunks

3½ oz (100 g) seeded orange segments

(about ½ medium fruit)

Preparation
In a blender, combine yogurt, pineapple, and orange.

Blend until smooth.

Simply Straw-banana

Makes 1 glass

Tried and true, the strawberry banana smoothie remains a favorite for many. The texture is smooth; the flavor is sweet.

Ingredients
1 cup frozen plain yogurt

5 oz (150 g) (about 1 cup) fresh strawberries

1¾ oz (50 g) banana slices (about ½ medium fruit)

Preparation
In a blender, combine yogurt, strawberries, and banana.

Blend until smooth.

Mediterranean Yogurt Shake

Makes 1 glass

This distinct smoothie includes tahini, dates, and pecans, along with frozen and fresh goat yogurt. Make sure you thoroughly blend the tahini with water before placing it in the blender. The pecans can be replaced with walnuts.

Ingredients

1–2 tablespoons tahini

1–2 tablespoons water

½ cup frozen plain goat yogurt

½ cup plain goat yogurt

1¾ oz (50 g) pitted dried dates (about 3 large fruit)

¼ cup chopped raw pecans

Preparation

In a small bowl, mix tahini with water until smooth. Transfer to a blender, and add frozen yogurt, yogurt, dates, and pecans. Blend until evenly combined.

White Watermelon Yogurt Surprise

Makes 2 glasses

This shake features an unexpected combination of frozen yogurt, fresh watermelon, and white chocolate. Chunky, sweet, and surprising!

Ingredients

1 cup frozen plain yogurt

5 oz (150 g) (about ¾ cup) seedless watermelon chunks

¼ cup white chocolate chips

Preparation

In a blender, combine yogurt, watermelon, and chocolate chips. Blend until evenly combined.

White Watermelon Yogurt Surprise

Tropical Low-fat Shake

Tropical Low-fat Shake

Makes 1 glass

With just two simple ingredients,
this shake is easy to make.

Ingredients

1 fat-free pineapple frozen pop, coarsely chopped

1 fat-free coconut vanilla yogurt

Preparation

In a blender, combine frozen pop and yogurt.

Blend until smooth.

Low-fat Pear-berry

Makes 1 glass

(see photo page 78)

So simple and flavorful, it's hard to believe
this smoothie has no fat.

Ingredients

7 oz (200 g) pear chunks (1–2 medium fruit)

½ cup frozen fat-free strawberry yogurt

Preparation

In a blender, combine pears and yogurt.

Blend until smooth.

Light Coco-Strawberry

Makes 1 glass

This smoothie has lots of flavor, color and taste. It calls for stevia, a herbal natural sweetener that is about 300 times sweeter than sugar, yet doesn't affect glucose levels. It can be replaced with another sweetener if you like.

Ingredients

5 oz (150 g) (about 1 cup) frozen strawberries

½ cup fat-free plain yogurt

½ teaspoon cocoa powder

1 serving stevia

Preparation

In a blender, combine strawberries, yogurt, cocoa powder, and stevia. Blend until smooth.

Guilt-free Choco-Banana

Makes 1 glass

This smoothie has the richness and flavor of chocolate, but is much lighter than most chocolate desserts.

Ingredients

3½ oz (100 g) frozen banana slices (about 1 medium fruit)

½ cup fat-free chocolate pudding

¼ cup low-fat milk

Preparation

In a blender, combine banana, pudding, and milk. Blend until smooth.

Guilt-free Choco-Banana

Low-fat Pear-berry (see recipe page 75)

Smoothies, Smoothies & More Smoothies!

Blueberry Pudding Shake (see recipe page 80)

Blueberry Pudding Shake

Makes 1 glass

(see photo page 79)

For a sweet creamy treat that can last an entire week, make a double batch of this smoothie, pour into an ice cube tray, and insert sticks into each cube.

Ingredients

1 cup frozen blueberries

½ cup fat-free vanilla pudding

Preparation

In a blender, combine blueberries and pudding.

Blend until smooth.

Lovingly Lemon

Makes 1 glass

With lemon and pineapple, this smoothie is light, refreshing, and easy to make!

Ingredients

1 fat-free lemon frozen pop, coarsely chopped

5 oz (150 g) (about 1 cup) chopped pineapple

¼ cup pineapple juice

Preparation

In a blender, combine frozen pop, pineapple, and pineapple juice. Blend until smooth.

Lovingly Lemon

Super Specials

Plush Plum

Makes 1 glass

This smoothie is best made with sweet rather than sour plums. Mixed with chocolate liqueur and coconut milk, the flavors harmonize wonderfully. If you like, serve in a margarita glass with a scoop of ice cream.

Ingredients

10 oz (300 g) plum chunks (about 3 to 4 medium fruit)

3 tablespoons chocolate liqueur

⅓ cup coconut milk

3 small ice cubes

Preparation

In a blender, combine plums, chocolate liqueur, coconut milk, and ice. Blend until smooth.

Choco-Tahini Shake

Makes 1 glass

Tahini, a thick paste made from sesame seeds, is often used in savory dishes. In this unique smoothie, it is combined with chocolate chips and banana for a marvelously smooth yet chunky texture.

Ingredients

4 scoops chocolate ice cream

3½ oz (100 g) frozen banana slices (about 1 medium fruit)

¼ cup dark chocolate chips

2 tablespoons tahini

Preparation

In a blender, combine ice cream, banana, chocolate chips, and tahini. Blend until evenly combined.

Choco-Tahini Shake

Hibiscus Harvest

Makes 1 glass

Ingredients

1 hibiscus teabag or 3 dried hibiscus flowers

3 tablespoons boiling water

5 oz (150 g) (about 1 cup) lychees, peeled and pitted

½ cup frozen plain yogurt

⅛ teaspoon rose water

¼ cup raw cashew nuts

1 teaspoon honey

4 small ice cubes

Preparation

Place hibiscus and boiling water in a small cup, and let it steep for 30 minutes. Strain tea, and pour 1 tablespoon of it into a blender. Add lychees, yogurt, rose water, cashew nuts, honey, and ice. Blend until evenly combined.

Bananango Breeze

Makes 1 glass

Nutty chestnuts combine with smooth banana, sweet mango, and tangy orange zest for a festival of scents and flavors.

Ingredients

3½ oz (100 g) frozen banana slices (about 1 medium fruit)

5 oz (150 g) (about 1¼ cups) mango chunks

1¾ oz (50 g) roasted chestnuts, chopped and peeled

¼ cup water, ¼ cup plain yogurt

Orange zest, 4 small ice cubes

Preparation

In a blender, combine banana, mango, chestnuts, water, yogurt, orange zest, and ice. Blend until evenly combined.

Bold Berry and Balsamic

Makes 1 glass

Ingredients

½ cup balsamic vinegar

1 tablespoon brown sugar

7 oz (200 g) (about 1½ cups) frozen strawberries

1 cup water

¼ cup chopped caramelized pecans

Preparation

Combine vinegar and sugar in a small saucepan, and bring
to a boil over medium-high heat. Continue to boil for several
minutes, until mixture reduces by half. Set aside to cool.
In a blender, combine strawberries, water, 1 tablespoon
of reduced vinegar, and caramelized pecans.
Blend until evenly combined.

Bold Berry and Balsamic

Spiked Raisin Surprise

Makes 1 glass

(see photo page 140)

Brandy-soaked raisins, creamy vanilla ice cream, nutty toasted seeds - combine these diverse flavors for a shake that's nutty, flavorful, and distinct.

Ingredients

1¾ oz (50 g) raisins

1–2 tablespoons brandy

4 scoops vanilla ice cream

1 teaspoon toasted sesame seeds

¼ cup milk

Preparation

In a small bowl, combine raisins with just enough brandy to cover. Let it stand for 1 hour. Transfer brandy-soaked raisins to a blender, and add ice cream, sesame seeds, and milk. Blend until evenly combined.

Choco Flake Shake

Makes 2 glasses

Lots of people love to start their day with cornflakes. Why not integrate them into a mid-morning snack as well? This smoothie combines cornflakes, ice cream, and toasted sesame seeds, for a smoothie that is nutty and unusual, yet comforting and rich.

Ingredients

6 scoops chocolate ice cream

1 cup cornflakes

1 tablespoon toasted sesame seeds

Preparation

In a blender, combine ice cream, cornflakes, and sesame seeds. Blend until evenly combined.

Choco Flake Shake

Spicy Rabbit

Spicy Rabbit

Makes 1 glass

This bold smoothie combines traditional smoothie
ingredients such as mangoes and carrot juice with just
the right amount of ground chili powder.
It's refreshing and vibrant!

Ingredients

½ cup carrot juice

5 oz (150 g) (about 1¼ cups) mango chunks

⅛ teaspoon ground chili powder

8 small ice cubes

Preparation

In a blender, combine carrot juice, mango, chili powder,
and ice. Blend until smooth.

Surprisingly Cilantro

Makes 1 glass

Mango and kiwi are a classic combination. The addition of
cilantro makes the smoothie magnificently surprising.

Ingredients

5 oz (150 g) kiwi chunks (about 1½ medium fruit)

5 oz (150 g) (about 1¼ cups) frozen mango chunks

Handful of cilantro leaves

Preparation

In a blender, combine kiwi, mango, and cilantro.
Blend until smooth.

Gracefully Guava

Makes 1 glass

People who like guava will be delighted to discover this distinct way of preparing them! If you leave seeds in the guavas, don't blend this smoothie too much, so that the seeds remain whole.

Ingredients

7 oz (200 g) guava chunks (about 2–3 medium fruit)

¾ cup plain yogurt

2 tablespoons maple syrup

1–2 tablespoons anise-flavored liqueur

4 small ice cubes

Preparation

In a blender, combine guava, yogurt, maple syrup, liqueur, and ice. Blend just until combined.

Melon Marmalade Medley

Makes 1 glass

Melon and marmalade may seem like unlikely bedfellows, but they make a magical team in this smoothie. Refreshing and sweet, it's perfect for serving at midday.

Ingredients

5 oz (150 g) pear chunks (about 1–2 medium fruit)

5 oz (150 g) (about 1 cup) honeydew chunks

2 tablespoons orange marmalade

Orange zest, to taste

4 small ice cubes

Preparation

In a blender, combine pears, honeydew, marmalade, orange zest, and ice. Blend until smooth.

Melon Marmalade Medley

Nutmeg Fig Shake

Makes 1 glass

(see photo page 96)

The rich flavor of fresh figs harmonizes perfectly with maple syrup and nutmeg in this smoothie. Make sure your ice cream is properly frozen before adding it to the blender.

Ingredients

3 scoops vanilla ice cream

5 oz (150 g) (about 1¼ cups) fresh figs

1 tablespoon maple syrup

Nutmeg, to taste

Preparation

In a blender, combine ice cream, figs, maple syrup and nutmeg. Blend until smooth.

Lusciously Lychee

Makes 1 glass

Very possibly perfect, this smoothie combines pineapple, lychees, and coconut milk with creamy vanilla ice cream. For just the right texture, make sure the ice cream goes directly from the freezer to the blender.

Ingredients

5 oz (150 g) (about 1 cup) frozen pineapple chunks

2½ oz (75 g) (about ½ cup) lychees, peeled and pitted

¼ cup coconut milk

1 scoop vanilla ice cream

Preparation

In a blender, combine pineapple, lychees, coconut milk, and ice cream. Blend until smooth.

Lusciously Lychee

Nutmeg Fig Shake (see recipe page 94)

Chai Masala Smoothie (see recipe page 98)

Chai Masala Smoothie

Makes 1 glass

(see photo page 97)

India's famous tea is combined with just the right amount of sugar, milk, and plenty of ice cubes, for a spicy and sweet chilled tea treat. If you don't have any chai tea at home, use strongly brewed black tea instead, and add cinnamon, cardamom, ginger, black pepper, and cloves.

Ingredients

1 chai teabag

¼ cup hot water

¼ cup milk

2–3 tablespoons sugar water (page 16)

10 small ice cubes

Preparation

Place chai teabag and boiling water in a small cup, and let steep for 30 minutes. Strain tea, and pour into a blender. Add milk, sugar water, and ice. Blend until smooth.

Waldorf Smoothie

Makes 1 glass

This smoothie is much like the beloved New York salad, minus the mayo. You'll need about 4 to 5 stalks of celery to make ¼ cup of celery juice.

Ingredients

2½ oz (75 g) (about ½ cup) frozen pineapple chunks

3½ oz (100 g) Granny Smith apple chunks (about 1 medium fruit)

¼ cup celery juice

¼ cup applesauce

5 raw pecans, chopped

6 small ice cubes

Preparation

In a blender, combine pineapple, apple, celery juice, applesauce, pecans, and ice. Blend until evenly combined.

Waldorf Smoothie

Vegetables, Please

Cran-apple Beet Treat

Makes 1 glass

Smooth applesauce, tart cranberries, and raw beet combine to give this smoothie an out-of-the-ordinary texture and color. It's lovely for serving in the winter, when fresh fruit may be hard to find.

Ingredients

1 cup applesauce

1¾ oz (50 g) raw beet (about ¼ small beet), peeled and sliced

¼ cup dried cranberries

1 teaspoon brown sugar

4 small ice cubes

Preparation

In a blender, combine applesauce, beet, cranberries, brown sugar, and ice. Blend until evenly combined.

Spicy Scarlet

Makes 1 glass

In this brightly-colored smoothie, the complement between Indian flavors and raw beet is invigorating. Use goat yogurt instead of sour cream, if you like.

Ingredients

7 oz (200 g) raw beet (about 1 medium beet), peeled and sliced

½ cup sour cream

1 teaspoon garam masala (or combined ground coriander, cumin, and cardamom)

6 small ice cubes

Preparation

In a blender, combine beet, sour cream, spices, and ice. Blend until smooth.

Spicy Scarlet

Spicy California Citrus

Spicy California Citrus

Makes 1 glass

Ingredients

3½ oz (100 g) ripe avocado chunks

7 oz (200 g) Lebanese cucumber chunks
(about 2 small cucumbers)

¼ cup soy milk

1–2 tablespoons orange marmalade

¼ teaspoon chili flakes

1 teaspoon fresh lemon juice

Salt, to taste

6 small ice cubes

Preparation

In a blender, combine avocado, cucumber, milk, marmalade,
chili flakes, lemon juice, salt, and ice. Blend until smooth.

Spinach Gazpacho

Makes 2 glasses

Ingredients

1 cup tomato juice

¼ cup chopped raw walnuts

4 semi-dried tomatoes

3 ½ oz (100 g) Lebanese cucumber chunks
(about 1 small cucumber)

1½ oz (40 g) fresh spinach

4 drops Tabasco

1 clove garlic, peeled

Salt and pepper

7 small ice cubes

Preparation

In a blender, combine tomato juice, walnuts, tomatoes,
cucumber, spinach, Tabasco, garlic, salt, pepper, and ice.
Blend until evenly combined.

Creatively Cardamom

Makes 2 glasses

Carrot and orange are standard smoothie fare; adding cardamom and honey upgrades your smoothie to something really special. If the honey you are using has solidified, dissolve it in a bit of warm water before adding to the blender.

Ingredients

½ cup carrot juice

7 oz (200 g) seeded orange segments (about 1 medium fruit)

¼ teaspoon cardamom

1–2 teaspoons honey

8 small ice cubes

Preparation

In a blender, combine carrot juice, orange, cardamom, honey, and ice. Blend until smooth.

Perfectly Pesto

Makes 1 glass

The pine nuts in this smoothie recall the nuttiness of fresh pesto. With spinach and tomatoes, it's like a fresh summertime salad, served in a glass.

Ingredients

½ cup frozen plain yogurt

1¾ oz (50 g) fresh spinach

¼ cup toasted pine nuts

¼ cup tomato juice

½ teaspoon dried tomato paste

Salt and pepper

Preparation

In a blender, combine frozen yogurt, spinach, pine nuts, tomato juice, tomato paste, salt, and pepper. Blend until evenly combined.

Perfectly Pesto

Ginger Salad Smoothie

Makes 1 glass

(see photo page 20)

This smoothie features the vitamin-rich and tangy combination of green apples, raw beets and celery. You'll need about 4 to 5 stalks of celery to make ¼ cup of celery juice. For a more concentrated flavor, replace the ice cubes with ½ cup of frozen apple juice.

Ingredients

10 oz (300 g) Granny Smith Apple chunks
(about 2 medium fruit)

5 oz (150 g) raw beet (about 1 small beet) peeled and sliced

¼ cup celery juice

1 teaspoon fresh ginger, peeled and grated

4 small ice cubes

Preparation

In a blender, combine apples, beet, celery juice, ginger, and ice. Blend until smooth.

Beet-iful Beet

Makes 1 glass

This smoothie has a gorgeous color and a super smoothie texture. If you don't have frozen yogurt on hand, use 1 cup of chilled yogurt instead for a deliciously thick beverage.

Ingredients

½ cup plain yogurt

½ cup frozen plain yogurt

1¾ oz (50 g) raw beet (about ¼ small beet), peeled and sliced

1 tablespoon honey

Preparation

In a blender, combine yogurt, frozen yogurt, beet, and honey. Blend until smooth.

Beet-iful Beet

Celemelon

Makes 1 glass

This refreshing and light smoothie contains fresh celery juice and melon. You'll need about 4 to 5 stalks of celery to make ¼ cup of celery juice.

Ingredients

7 oz (200 g) (about 1½ cups) honeydew chunks

¼ cup celery juice

Salt, to taste

4 small ice cubes

Preparation

In a blender, combine honeydew, celery juice, salt, and ice. Blend until smooth.

Tabasco Gazpacho

Makes 2 glasses

Ingredients

1 cup tomato juice, 7 oz (200 g) Lebanese cucumber chunks (about 2 small cucumbers)

1 red bell pepper, seeded and chopped

2 tablespoons fresh lemon juice

Handful of parsley leaves

1 clove garlic

5 drops Tabasco

Salt and pepper

Preparation

In a blender, combine tomato juice, cucumber, pepper, lemon juice, parsley, garlic, Tabasco, salt, and pepper. Blend until evenly combined.

Tabasco Gazpacho

For Dessert

PB & Chocolate Shake

Makes 1 glass

Organization is important in this smoothie.
Put the ice cream in the bottom and the candy-coated
chocolate on top. Don't over-blend, since you want to
preserve a pleasant crunchy texture.

Ingredients

3 scoops vanilla ice cream

½ cup coconut milk

2 tablespoons peanut butter

¼ cup candy-coated chocolates

Preparation

In a blender, combine ice cream, coconut milk, peanut
butter, and chocolates. Blend until evenly combined.

Cheesecake Smoothie

Makes 1 glass

This smoothie is perfect for someone who is sweet on
cheesecake. If you like, serve this smoothie in a dessert
bowl, and reserve the jam for garnish. The jam can also be
stirred in with a spoon, to add a decorative swirl.

Ingredients

2¾ oz (80 g) butter cookies, coarsely chopped

4 oz (120 g) cream cheese

2 tablespoons brown sugar

1 tablespoon strawberry, cherry, or raspberry jam

1 cup milk

Preparation

In a blender, combine cookies, cream cheese, brown sugar,
jam, and milk. Blend until evenly combined.

Cheesecake Smoothie

Cookie Frappe

Makes 1 glass

Many people love having cookies with their coffee. This smoothie blends the cookies right into the coffee, along with vanilla ice cream for good measure!

Ingredients

1 teaspoon instant coffee

1 tablespoon boiling water

4 cream-filled chocolate sandwich cookies, coarsely chopped

4 scoops vanilla ice cream

4 small ice cubes

½ cup milk

Preparation

Dissolve instant coffee in water and let it cool. In a blender, combine cooled coffee, cookies, ice cream, ice, and milk. Blend until evenly combined.

Chocolate Frappe

Makes 1 glass

What's better than a cup of coffee for chasing away the mid-morning blues?
How about a coffee-banana-chocolate smoothie?

Ingredients

1–2 teaspoons instant coffee

1 tablespoon boiling water

3½ oz (100 g) frozen banana slices (about 1 medium fruit)

¾ cup milk

¼ cup dark chocolate chips

¼ cup white chocolate chips

Preparation

Dissolve instant coffee in water and let it cool. In a blender, combine cooled coffee, banana, milk, and chocolate chips. Blend until evenly combined.

Chocolate Frappe

Hazelnut Orange Shake

Hazelnut Orange Shake

Makes 1 glass

This smoothie blends the classic flavors of chocolate, hazelnut, and orange. It's sweet, rich, and nutty, a perfect craving satisfier.

Ingredients

4 scoops chocolate ice cream

½ cup chopped roasted hazelnuts

½ cup milk

1 tablespoon orange marmalade

Preparation

In a blender, combine ice cream, hazelnuts, milk, and marmalade. Blend until evenly combined.

Nutty Nut Shake

Makes 1 glass

Nut lovers will go crazy for this nutty smoothie. With just the right balance of chocolate and banana flavors, it's flavorful and filling. If you don't have banana ice cream in the freezer, replace it with 1 frozen banana and 2 scoops of vanilla ice cream.

Ingredients

4 scoops banana ice cream

2 tablespoons chocolate-hazelnut spread

¼ cup chopped caramelized pecans

¼ cup milk

Preparation

In a blender, combine ice cream, chocolate-hazelnut spread, pecans, and milk. Blend until evenly combined.

Nougat Nibbler

Makes 1 glass

This delicious smoothie will satisfy the hungriest sweet tooth. Make sure the ice cream is properly frozen. You can use a frozen banana if you like, but you may need to add a bit more milk.

Ingredients

4 scoops vanilla ice cream

½ cup milk

One 2-ounce (60 gram) peanut nougat chocolate bar, coarsely chopped

3½ oz (100 g) banana slices (about 1 medium fruit)

Preparation

In a blender, combine ice cream, milk, chocolate bar, and banana. Blend until evenly combined.

Strawberry Cookie

Makes 1 glass

If you don't have strawberry frozen yogurt, use ½ cup frozen yogurt and 3½ oz (100 g) frozen strawberries instead.

Ingredients

4 scoops strawberry frozen yogurt

4 cream-filled chocolate sandwich cookies, coarsely chopped

½ cup milk

Preparation

In a blender, combine frozen yogurt, cookies, and milk. Blend until evenly combined.

Strawberry Cookie

Strawberry Sundae

Strawberry Sundae

Makes 1 glass

This milkshake-style smoothie is a great summertime dessert. If you're crazy about strawberries, replace the vanilla ice cream with strawberry ice cream, and garnish with fresh strawberries.

Ingredients

2 scoops strawberry ice cream

2 scoops vanilla ice cream

½ cup milk

1–2 tablespoons caramel syrup

Preparation

In a blender, combine strawberry ice cream, vanilla ice cream, milk, and caramel syrup. Blend until smooth.

Coconut Craze

Makes 1 glass

This smoothie is like a blended coconut sundae.
If you like, replace the candy-coated peanuts with
candy-coated chocolates.

Ingredients

4 scoops chocolate ice cream

½ cup coconut milk

2 tablespoons shredded coconut

1¾ oz (50 g) candy-coated peanuts

Preparation

In a blender, combine ice cream, coconut milk, coconut,
and candy-coated peanuts. Blend until evenly combined.

Papayan Paradise

Makes 1 glass

This decadent smoothie contains caramelized pecans,
chocolate, and coconut cream. The addition of papaya
imbues it with unexpected flavor and color.

Ingredients

8½ oz (about 250 g) (about 2 cups) papaya chunks

¼ cup coconut cream

¼ cup chopped caramelized pecans

¼ cup white chocolate chips

6 small ice cubes

Preparation

In a blender, combine papaya, coconut cream,
caramelized pecans, chocolate chips, and ice.
Blend until evenly combined.

Nutty Strawberry Smoothie

Makes 2 glasses

Strawberries, cream, and caramelized pecans — that's all you need for a fruity and decadent treat. This smoothie is perfect for serving when strawberry season is over, since it contains frozen berries.

Ingredients

5 oz (150 g) (about 1 cup) frozen strawberries

¾ cup plain yogurt

2 tablespoons cream cheese

¼ cup chopped caramelized pecans

1–2 teaspoons brown sugar

Preparation

In a blender, combine strawberries, yogurt, cream cheese, pecans, and brown sugar. Blend until evenly combined.

White Chocolate Berry-licious

Makes 1 glass

The white chocolate in this smoothie makes it extra smooth, creamy, and rich. It makes a great decadent treat or a well-deserved dessert. Serve it at your next dinner party for an elegant indulgence

---

Ingredients

1 cup strawberry yogurt

¼ cup frozen raspberries

¼ cup frozen blueberries

¼ cup white chocolate chips

Preparation

In a blender, combine yogurt, raspberries, blueberries, and chocolate chips. Blend until evenly combined.

White Chocolate Berry-licious

PB & J

Makes 1 glass

Take the classic sandwich combo of peanut butter and jelly, lose the bread, add a frozen banana, and blend it all together. Serve at lunchtime — or any time!

Ingredients

7 oz (200 g) frozen banana slices (about 2 medium fruit)

2 tablespoons peanut butter

1–2 tablespoons strawberry jelly

½ cup milk

Preparation

In a blender, combine bananas, peanut butter, jelly, and milk. Blend until smooth.

PB & Banana

Makes 1 glass

Love to indulge in peanut butter and banana sandwiches? How about blending it all together, along with chocolate chips and a cool glass of milk? Peanut perfection!

Ingredients

3½ oz (100 g) frozen banana slices (about 1 medium fruit)

¾ cup milk

2 tablespoons peanut butter

¼ cup dark chocolate chips

Preparation

In a blender, combine banana, milk, peanut butter, and chocolate chips. Blend until evenly blended.

PB & Banana

Cocktail Hour

Delicate Daiquiri

Makes 1 glass

Light, delicate, and delicious, this smoothie makes
a lovely finish to an indulgent lunch. It's perfect
for serving at summertime barbecues.

Ingredients

¼ cup (50 ml) rum

2 tablespoons triple sec

5 oz (150 g) (about 1 cup) frozen honeydew chunks

3½ oz (100 g) (about ¾ cup) lychees, peeled and pitted

2 tablespoons fresh lemon juice

2 tablespoons sugar water (page 16)

Preparation

In a blender, combine, rum, triple sec, honeydew, lychees,
lemon juice, and sugar water. Blend until smooth.

Daiqui-kiwi

Makes 1 glass

If you favor kiwis and rum, this cocktail can't be beaten.
It is refreshingly tangy and packs just the right
amount of punch.

Ingredients

¼ cup (50 ml) rum

2 tablespoons triple sec

5 oz (150 g) kiwi chunks (about 1½ medium fruit)

1 tablespoon fresh lemon juice

2 tablespoons sugar water (page 16)

1 teaspoon grenadine

10 small ice cubes

Preparation

In a blender, combine rum, triple sec, kiwi, lemon juice,
sugar water, grenadine, and ice. Blend until smooth.

Daiqui-kiwi

Pink Herb Daiquiri

Pink Herb Daiquiri

Makes 1 glass

Strawberries go well with a variety of herbs, and basil is no exception. This pretty beverage is refreshing in flavor and color!

Ingredients

7 oz (200 g) (about 1½ cups) frozen strawberries

¼ cup (50 ml) rum

2 tablespoons triple sec

1 tablespoon lemon juice

2 tablespoons sugar water (page 16)

3 basil leaves

Preparation

In a blender, combine strawberries, rum, triple sec, lemon juice, sugar water, and basil. Blend until smooth.

Spiked Bananas

Makes 1 glass

This cocktail strikes a balance between the smooth sweetness of banana and the sharp tanginess of lemon. It's temptingly easy to drink, too.

Ingredients

¼ cup (50 ml) vodka

3½ oz (100 g) frozen sliced banana (about 1 medium fruit)

2 tablespoons fresh lemon juice

2 tablespoons sugar water (page 16)

8 small ice cubes

Preparation

In a blender, combine vodka, banana, lemon juice, sugar water, and ice. Blend until smooth.

Fig Ambrosia

Makes 1 glass

With fig liqueur and frozen grapes, this smoothie is fit to feed angels. You can use either green or red grapes for this drink, just make sure they are seedless. As a garnish, serve additional frozen grapes on the side.

Ingredients

9 oz (250 g) (about 1½ cups) frozen seedless grapes

¼ cup (50 ml) fig liqueur

1 tablespoon lime juice

1 teaspoon grenadine

Preparation

In a blender, combine grapes, liqueur, lime juice, and grenadine. Blend until smooth.

Frozen Cran Cosmo

Makes 1 glass

This version of the beloved cosmopolitan cocktail features frozen cranberries and ice.

Ingredients

¼ cup (50 ml) citrus vodka

1 cup frozen cranberries

Lemon zest, to taste

2 tablespoons sugar water (page 16)

6 small ice cubes

Preparation

In a blender, combine vodka, cranberries, lemon zest, sugar water, and ice. Blend until smooth.

Frozen Cran Cosmo

Passion-ita

Passion-ita

Makes 1 glass

This tropical frozen margarita features the sweet
and sour flavors of passion fruit and lemon juice.
It looks gorgeous and tastes even better!

Ingredients

2½ oz (70 g) passion fruit (about 2–3 medium fruit), halved

¼ cup (50 ml) tequila

2 tablespoons triple sec

1 tablespoon fresh lemon juice

3 tablespoons sugar water (page 16)

10 small ice cubes

Preparation

Scoop out contents of passion fruit, and transfer to a
blender. Add tequila, triple sec, lemon juice, sugar water,
and ice. Blend until evenly combined.

Spiked Watermelon

Makes 2 glasses

You'll need frozen watermelon to get just the right
texture for this fun, fruity cocktail.

Ingredients

¼ cup (50 ml) vodka

9 oz (250 g) (about 1½ cups) frozen watermelon chunks

2 tablespoons fresh lemon juice

2 tablespoons sugar water (page 16)

Preparation

In a blender, combine vodka, watermelon, lemon juice,
and sugar water. Blend until smooth.

Whisky-a-Cho-Co

Whisky-a-Cho-Co

Makes 1 glass

The surprising combination of ingredients in this drink
will take your breath away. Delicious and satisfying,
a single recipe is just right for serving two, so invite
a good friend over and share.

Ingredients

4 scoops chocolate ice cream

¼ cup (50 ml) whisky

¼ cup dark chocolate chips

Chili flakes, to taste

6 small ice cubes

Preparation

In a blender, combine ice cream, whisky, chocolate chips,
chili flakes, and ice. Blend until evenly combined.

Bittersweet Symphony

Makes 1 glass

This smoothie is just right for people who like bitter drinks.
A simple blend of Campari, mango, and ice — the result
is a symphony of flavor.

Ingredients

¼ cup (40 ml) Campari

5 oz (150 g) (about 1¼ cups) mango chunks

6 small ice cubes

Preparation

In a blender, combine Campari, mango, and ice.
Blend until smooth.

Spiked Raisin Surprise (see recipe page 88)

Index